Edited by Chris Charlesworth.
Book designed by Michael Bell Design.
Picture research by Nicola Russell.

ISBN 0.7119.4810.0
Order No. OP47744

Exclusive Distributors:
Book Sales Limited,
8/9 Frith Street,
London W1V 5TZ, UK.

Music Sales Corporation,
257 Park Avenue South,
New York, NY 10010, USA.

Music Sales Pty Limited,
120 Rothschild Avenue, Rosebery,
NSW 2018, Australia.

To the Music Trade only:
Music Sales Limited,
8/9 Frith Street,
London W1V 5TZ, UK.

Photo credits:
Cover: Front/Derek Ridgers; Back/Sandra Johnson.
All Action: 4b,51bl; Greg Allen/Retna:17b,
51t; D.Anderson/SIN: 16; A.J.Barrett/Retna:
46t,47tr&bl; Jay Blakesberg/Retna: 48m;
Anita Bugge/SIN: 53t; Chris Carroll/Retna: 61;
Chris Cuffaro/Katz: 55b,58; Bernard Dexter/
Retna: 24tr; Henry Diltz/Retna: 14t,23b,51m;
Steve Double/Retna: 46b; Cheryl Dunn/Retna:
18b,19,24b; Famous: 33,56bl&r,59t,60tl,
62tl; Brad Fierce/Katz: 29; M.Goodacre/SIN: 59b;
Sandra Johnson /Retna: 7,42t; Michael Linssen/
Redferns: 23t,27l,43b,44t; London Features
International: 1,4t,8,9,10,11t,11b,12,13,
17t,18t,21,24tl,25,26,30,31,36,37b,42b,49,
51br,54,56tl,57,60br,60tr,63,64; Frank
Micelotta/Katz: 52; Karen Miller/Retna: 45;
Tony Mott/SIN: 22; Paul Natkin/Katz: 47tl;
Katia Natola/SIN: 39; Neal Preston/Retna:
44b; Relay: 6,15,36b,41tl,43t,48t,48b;
Clemens Rikken/Retna: 37t; Ebet Roberts/
Redferns: 14b,28,32,34,35,40,41br,54b;
Rex Features: 20t,20b,27b,38b,50,53b,55t,
56tr,62bl&r; S.Starr/Katz: 5.

Printed in the United Kingdom by
Ebenezer Baylis & Son Limited, Worcester.

M000025465

RED CH PEPP

Sex, surf, scandal. Agony, ecstasy, extremes. Where the abnormal is the norm. Los Angeles, the city of angels, the ultimate metropolis, where modern life screams along at breakneck speed and flies off the rails every second of every day. But what of Los Angeles' rich culture, the multi-cultural population, the art galleries, the Getty Museum, the hundreds of other examples of its fabulous history. The millions of tourists who flock to the city every year are not interested in this cultural backdrop – they want the film stars, the glamour, the celluloid scandal and the public immorality. Then, when the city is crumbling in its own embers, the same people will dismiss Los Angeles as an inevitable victim of its own decadence, the result of too much drink, too many drugs, too much sex and too much scandal. Just too much.

When the Red Hot Chili Peppers lead singer Anthony Kiedis was convicted of sexual battery and indecent exposure in 1990, the general consensus was a frowning 'he got what he deserved'. The same judgements were murmured when bassist Flea was arrested for various misdemeanours in 1991, and thus at every stage of their riotous and controversial career the Chili Peppers have been chastised for what

HOT ILLI PERS

Spike Harvey

the self-appointed moral guardians see as unsavoury and unsociable behaviour. And yet at every same stage the music was almost a forgotten guest, a bystander to the whirlpool of events and incidents that besieged the band, some self-induced, others imposed, events that eventually cost them the life of one member and the mental collapse of another. The press picked at the corpse of their scandal whilst a feast of music lay untouched next to the scavenging hordes.

Untouched, that is, until 1991 and the landmark album 'Bloodsugarsexmagik'. Despite the continued mainstream radio rejections and the conventional distaste and dismissal of 'unfashionable' funk, the Red Hot Chili Peppers smashed into the top of the US album charts, where their fifth long player stayed for over a year, achieving triple platinum status and catapulting the band into the higher

echelons of the world's top groups. Some might say it was sorely misplaced derivative nostalgia played by sexist meatheads completely undeserving of any credit. Those same people probably go to Los Angeles and head straight for Disneyland.

Melbourne, Australia, the capital of Victoria state, built on gold rushes and the river Yarra. Some thirty years before the Chili Peppers took the world to one side and funked it to death, Michael Balzary was born. Five years later his parents divorced and he headed with his mother for the twentieth century's very own eternal gold rush, New York city. After a brief stay in the Big Apple, the family made their way to Los Angeles where the young Michael's mother re-married a respected jazz musician called Walter Urban Jr.

The awkwardness and resentment that scars so many step-relations never reared its ugly head here however – Michael and Walter gelled immediately and the youngster frequently found himself jamming with the wealth of musical talent that dropped by his house every week to play out their melodic obsessions with his step-father. The fascination that the young boy developed for this music helped to bring him out of his shell, and gradually eroded the chronic shyness which had been something of a worrying feature of his early years. By the time he went to High School he was a confident, if somewhat unusual, character. When he arrived at school his musical tastes alienated him from his peers, as he found all his friends were listening to disco and the sound of the dancefloor. With his unusual appearance and his odd, mixed up accent, as well as his highly individual musical tastes, Michael was regularly picked upon, and one kid in particular seemed to be the chief perpetrator, Jack Irons. Michael, now nick-named Flea, couldn't get home quick enough to play his records by Miles Davis, Ornette Coleman and Dizzy Gillespie. Once he picked up a trumpet and began to mimic the masters, the fascination really grew – one night when his mother introduced him to Dizzy Gillespie backstage at a gig, he stood for fifteen minutes and talked to the great legend, the same man he had copied and listened to in awe for hour after hour in his bedroom every week. Then he heard his first funk records, and he was hooked – the jazz legends were delicately placed at the back of his collection as his funk interests grew. Pretty soon he was something of an expert aficionado, and was already showing excellent musical ability. His eager interest became a genuine and compulsive love.

Anthony Kiedis' first draw on a joint was with his Dad. He lost his virginity aged 12 to one of the many women who passed through his father's apartment. By the age of 15 he had experimented with a range of drugs and slept with a gaggle of women. This was all very different to the staid middle-class life he had lived up until the age of 11 with his doting mother in Grand Rapids, a predominantly Dutch area of Michigan. Every summer he would visit his divorced father, a small time actor who used the stage name Blackie Dammett. Back in Michigan, Anthony had become something of a roughneck hooligan, so what he saw when he arrived each year in Los Angeles thrilled him – he soaked up the Bohemian atmosphere of anything goes. Once the decision was made to live with Blackie permanently, Anthony was just about ready to try anything that came his way. Such was his father's love of the high life that Anthony frequently had to turn for company to the singer Sonny Bono, a family friend who was himself still reeling from the acrimonious break-up of his marriage to his musical and matrimonial partner Cher. For a teenager to be in an environment where there were no limits, it was a wild and decadent time – it would take Kiedis some time before he finally, and painfully, discovered his own personal limits.

In 1977 Kiedis started at Fairfax High School in Hollywood. Bearing in mind his band's later success, he could scarcely have had a better apprenticeship – amongst Fairfax's prestigious list of former pupils were none other than Phil Spector, Jerry Lieber and Herb Alpert. One day when he saw one of his best friends being beaten up he stepped into the fray and found himself standing opposite an odd looking character called Flea. Despite having met so strangely, the two struck up a close and wild friendship, and proceeded to become something of school legends for their anarchic behaviour. One such habit was their suicidal taste for jumping from tall buildings into swimming pools – on one occasion Kiedis missed and bounced off the concrete before flopping into the pool, his back fractured. Undeterred, the two 15-year-olds continued their hectic lifestyle.

Pretty soon bands were being formed and Flea's obvious talent and encyclopedic knowledge meant that he was a much sought after recruit for various school combos. One such band was Anthym, whose founder members were boys called Hillel Slovak and Flea's erstwhile tormentor, Jack Irons. Slovak was born in Haifa in Israel and, like Kiedis and Flea, he experienced upheaval at the tender age of five, when his family moved to LA, where, along with his best friend and native Californian Irons, he became enamoured of Kiss. The two pals even formed their own Kiss mime act. Once these early musical projects had evolved into something more substantial, Slovak became obsessed with Jimi Hendrix, and his own guitar style developed dramatically.

The band's unity was destined to end prematurely however, when Flea left to join seminal LA punksters Fear, whose manic singer Lee Ving led a band notorious for violent shows and outrageous behaviour. At the same time Flea also delved into the acting world with a small role as a fledgling punk in a Penelope Spheeris' film of disaffected youth called *Suburbia*. Slovak and Irons stayed together with Anthym but renamed themselves What Is This?, a highly appropriate name for a band with a bewildering range of styles varying from punk to funk and everything in between. The four friends went their separate ways for some time before being asked to play a guest spot at a friend's gig at the local Rhythm Lounge Club. A week before the

Before that next gig they had ren⸱ the band The Red Hot Chili Peppers⸱ they maintain to this day they found 'a psychedelic bush in the Hollywood Whatever its origin, it was a name th⸱ was on everybody's lips in the area o⸱ the next twelve months. Realising the⸱ had stumbled onto something unique, Peppers began gigging prolifically, eve⸱ though Flea, Slovak and Irons continue⸱ their involvement in other bands for sc⸱ time to come. It was the autumn of 19⸱ and within three months they were the hottest band on the circuit. The music rapidly shaped itself into an amalgam of punk and funk that was both highly unfashionable and incredibly powerful. The various influences of the band manifested themselves in a compelling way. Flea had seen the hardcore of Black Flag but was unimpressed; Kiedis and Slovak loved it. Kiedis in particular loved the connection it made between the

Soon after the two friends formed the garage punk band Anthym and recruited Flea, who by now had become something of an accomplished bassist. After a shaky start, they slowly progressed until, by 1980, they had worked their way onto the Hollywood club circuit, where nervous club owners hid them in the back rooms until show time because they were too young to even gain entry into these venues. They earned a very small, but vocal following locally, and nobody was more vocal than one kid who was at every gig – Anthony Kiedis. Kiedis meantime had been writing poetry and living the high life at his father's apartment. When it was suggested that Kiedis became involved with Anthym he jumped at the chance, but only really for fun, as an emcee, reciting some of his off the wall poetry before introducing the band to the bemused audiences.

show all they had was a funky bassline of Flea's and a poem by Kiedis, but they filled their heads with acid and went on stage anyway, under the moniker of Tony Flow and The Miraculously Majestic Masters of Mayhem. Their impromptu performance of 'Out In LA' became local folklore within days of the foursome stepping offstage. Amid their laughs and general joviality after the mini-gig, the four could not have imagined what was about to happen – within six months they were signed to an eight album recording deal with EMI America. Their first gig together had been a joke – the next time they played there were queues around the block.

music and the soul, making people react and hitting them in the gut – he knew then that one day he wanted to be able to do the same with the music he was involved in. Flea by now was a veritable funk expert, and being the bass player this stamped an indelible footprint all over their musical work. Kiedis began to listen to rap and this moulded his vocal style, already at times a harsh and captivating howl, and by now had adopted the alias o⸱ Anton The Swan. Once the members had discovered bands such as Funkadelic, Parliament and Defunkt, they were well and truly set on a road that was highly individual at a time when such music wa⸱ almost commercially forgotten since its heyday in the Seventies.

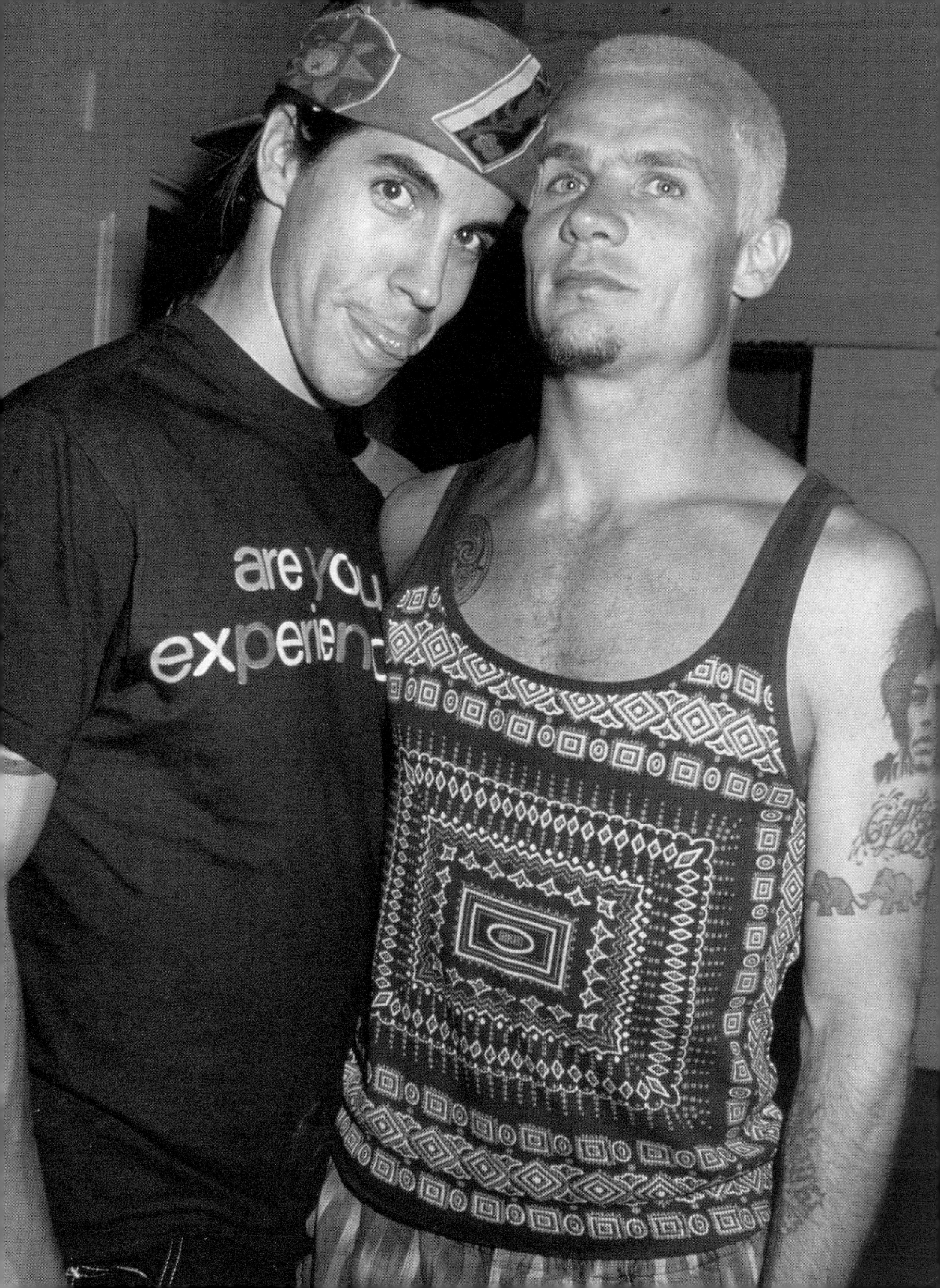
are you
experien

The four shared an apartment where they all lived at various stages, they played loads of gigs, anywhere for anything, and gave off an attitude of not caring what people thought or said. This was their thing and nobody was going to dampen it. Their live set, although still very raw, was manic, frenetic and exhausting to watch. They exuded sex and the deranged combo represented a demented visual act. Coupled with their unusual musical vision, this meant that the record companies flocked to see them, including EMI.

They gigged prolifically. They played a residency at the Cathay Grand Club. They played their first out of town show in the pretentious resort of Aspen, and were promptly sent packing with the promoter telling them never to bring their 'black' music back to offend his clients. But these early incidents paled into insignificance compared to a gig at a strip joint called the Kit Kat, where curvaceous naked female dancers cavorted around the stage as the band played. Having been used to near total attention up until now, the Chili Peppers were not happy to have the spotlight and focus on someone other than themselves when they were playing. After a subdued set, they returned for the encore of Jimi Hendrix's 'Fire' stark naked but for a sock over their genitals. Needless to say it attracted the attention of the crowd and word spread about this outrageous act. In many senses it was an inadvertently brilliant piece of marketing; in another sense, it was possibly a very big mistake. When the punters left that night, everyone was talking about 'the socks on cocks routine'. Nobody mentioned the music.

Nevertheless, with the EMI deal signed, Flea left Fear and joined the Chili Peppers full time, and on the way turned down John Lydon's request that he join PiL. All was going so well, they seemed unstoppable. Then EMI pointed out that Slovak and Irons had in fact contractual obligations with What Is This? that disallowed their involvement with both bands – they had to make a choice. They chose What Is This? Flea was disappointed; Kiedis was devastated. Slovak and Irons had been in the former band for six years, so it was understandable that they chose the way they did. Even so, it was a severe blow for the new band, barely out of its infancy. EMI graciously gave the stunned Chili Peppers several months to regroup before recording their début album. With the onus now firmly on Kiedis and Flea, the two friends recruited Jack Sherman on guitar and drummer Cliff Martinez, who had previously played in Lydia Lunch's 13.13 and Captain Beefheart and The Weirdos.

When it had become apparent that The Red Hot Chili Peppers were indeed going to be a feature of Californian music at the very least, Flea and Kiedis formulated a jovial, yet half-serious, vision for their band. It consisted of three logical steps: make their first record a great record; secondly, make a great video; and thirdly play a great tour. Their eponymously titled début album unfortunately did not prove to be the first of these steps. Produced by England's Andy Gill, from the influential Gang Of Four, the album was a difficult project from start to finish. For one, the band were still novices in recording studios, and they also had two new members who had only recently been welcomed into the fold with a small tour just prior to the album sessions. Secondly, and more problematic, was the poor relationship that developed between Gill and the band, which was civil at best, and dysfunctional the rest of the time.

It was the first time Gill had produced anyone outside of The Gang Of Four, and the band were immediately dismayed when he told them that the records he had made and which they so revered, were in fact 'bought by a few lunatics only' and that he held little respect for them himself. Thirdly, he now veered sharply away from the funk-punk revolutionary rhetoric of his old band and was now heading towards pop and radio music. This was wildly at odds with what the Chili Peppers were looking for and the strained circumstances were unlikely to result in a good record. At one stage, it is rumoured that Flea and Kiedis delivered a human turd in a pizza box to Gill at the mixing desk because he had been

overtures to recording music more suitable for radio play. The band wanted the raw funkiness of The Gang Of Four, mixing that group's sparse textures with their own unique power. They wanted to be proponents of hardcore, bone-crunching mayhem sex music but Gill was just not interested.

Whatever the reasons, it was an irreconcilable clash and many was the night that they squabbled deep into the small hours. Consequently, when the album was finally released, neither party was satisfied, and producer and band parted company with no desire to meet up again. It was a somewhat inglorious start to a recording career initiated by a hitherto bewildering series of live successes. Even so, the album was the first step of sorts – it was closer to avante-garde funk than any of the Chili Peppers later offerings, and in some cases was hard listening, but they had nevertheless signalled their intent. The influences of Parliament and Stax and Funkadelic were predominant and most tracks were built around Flea's by-now astonishing bass guitar abilities, but there was also an anarchistic, wild edge that the band had drawn from West Coast punk and East Coast hardcore, which made them sound like no other band around. Despite its many flaws, 'Red Hot Chili Peppers' as a début LP was a sign that here might be a band with the very real potential of creating a truly modern sound all of their own.

Sales of the album were very low indeed, but they were not disheartened, and in October they headed out for their first small headline tour of the States, although the dates were concentrated mainly on the West Coast and in the major mid-western cities. Live, unlike on record, there were no such problems, and the band were by now establishing something of an awesome reputation for their shows. With manager Lindy Goetz on board, the gigs began to flow thick and fast, and the Peppers played every one. With memories of the tension of the début album lingering, together with less than comfortable touring conditions, these were fraught times for the band, who travelled in a small van and suffered poor accommodation at most venues.

More worryingly, it became apparent that Jack Sherman was not fitting in with the other members, especially Flea and Kiedis who would be out on the town most nights whilst Sherman would stay in and relax. Since the Chili Peppers had been established on a foundation of friendship and kinship between the members, it was clearly a situation that could not continue. By January 1984 he was asked to leave, and Flea and Kiedis immediately began wooing their old friend Hillel Slovak to re-join.

What Is This? had failed to capitalise on their early success to the same degree as the Chili Peppers and as such, by the time Sherman left, they were effectively in stasis. Eventually, after much deliberation, Slovak decided to leave the band for good and hook up with his two friends in the Chili Peppers once again. Another worrying matter for the band during this period was their drug use. They had all experimented for many years; however, while Flea had lost interest and only dabbled occasionally, Kiedis and Slovak both began taking substantial quantities of heavy drugs around this time. Slovak denied the use, Kiedis didn't, but both continued regardless. The tour lifestyle and the outrageous characters of the band only served to encourage the tendency.

James Brown may be the commercially acknowledged master of funk, but nobody lives for the funk like George Clinton, mainman of Funkadelic, Parliament and various future permutations of the two, such as The P-Funk All Stars. Born in 1947, Clinton started off life as a hairdresser, but all that changed in 1967 when his first band Parliament had a US Top 20 hit with '(I Just Want To) Testify', a Motown style late Sixties sound that captivated the nation. Eventually his band transmuted into combinations of musicians, all phenomenally talented, and then in 1978 he enjoyed an Indian summer success with the track 'One Nation Under A Groove' which saw him play stadium tours across the States. Since then however, his career, like that of funk, had been quiet, unfashionable and ignored, even derided.

Not by the Chili Peppers though – to them funk was a religion and they worshipped at the altar of Dr. Clinton Funkenstein. That's why they asked him to produce their second album. He accepted and invited them to his country retreat studios outside Detroit, where they wrote and recorded thirteen songs. On the album, entitled 'Freaky Styley', Clinton introduced the superb musical skills of horn players like Maceo Parker and Fred Wesley, both Clinton sidemen who had won much fame through their work with James Brown in the Seventies. Alongside the Chili Peppers' original compositions, Clinton completed the soul connection with two cover versions, Sly Stone's US No.1 hit 'If You Want Me To Stay', and an old Meters' song 'Africa' which was modified to 'Hollywood (Africa)' when it was released as the first single from the album. The days were spent in the idyllic surroundings of Clinton's studio, chilling out with the man (whose real life character was notably more subdued than his manic stage persona), then the evenings would see the band plunge into the crazy nightlife of downtown Detroit. Studio techniques were much more relaxed than the strenuous first record – no click tracks were used for example; instead Clinton would dance around the studio, clapping and clicking his fingers and shouting 'Yeah, kick it, throw it down!!', while the band watched, amazed. The product of all this was a blatantly lustful album that displayed more than ever that funk music and sex were synonymous. With titles like 'Sex Rap', 'Thirty Dirty Birds' and 'Blackeyed Blonde' the band did not appear to wish to hide this either. Clinton leant the record a maturity and stopped the band's use of funk for funk's sake. It was a much more mature outing than their début, and the band and producer alike were very pleased with the result.

a single. The Chili Peppers remained a band of two different sides – an incredible, vital live phenomenon against what at this stage was no more than an interesting excursion into musical fusions on record.

In typical style, the tour for the album was lengthy and superb. Much of their following remained the fraternity element who liked the band's homo-erotic escapades and the bravado of their antics, and there were signs that the fan base was spreading. They played their first overseas show on this tour, at a German festival, where they also joined Clinton for a TV appearance before flying to the UK for a début one-off show. Back in the States, Martinez's membership of the band finally, and not unexpectedly, was terminated and Jack Irons re-joined on drums – they now had the original line-up restored and the live show was a colossus as a result. Having graduated onto the larger national circuit now, (including shows with Run DMC) the band plunged into a monster of a tour throughout the winter of 1985, which saw them spread the funk gospel far and wide.

'Freaky Styley' was an apocalyptic fusion of dance and hardcore, a record of extremes and one which maybe in retrospect had too much of Clinton's unique stamp on it. The Chili Peppers received wider recognition as a result of the album's small, but well-received sales, and in some areas were already seen as true pioneers. The problem now was that they had something of an identity crisis, and were in danger of becoming one of those seminal bands whose musical innovation and influence is exploited commercially by other, later acts.

The main weakness of the record was the lack of physical presence of the band – their live shows were all about that one word: physical. They were one of the nation's most frantic acts, bass thumping and guitars raging, but Clinton never saw them live and consequently there was an absence of that live energy on vinyl. And in many senses, without the sheer physical, sexual element that their gigs present, the Chili Peppers are nothing. Maybe allowing the mixing engineer to complete the final mix down without Clinton and the band being present was a mistake. Maybe. Whatever the reasons, it was a good progression, but a flawed one. Still no album had been released in Britain, and only a handful of European territories had received

The rigours of touring are hard enough, but when a band play every show as physically as the Chili Peppers, the demands of the lifestyle are enormous. Increasingly, Kiedis and Slovak turned to drugs to fuel their fire. The band were in many senses much like one of their heroes – Sly Stone. They vocalised many issues with their music, and were clearly a conscientious group of individuals, yet at times they appeared to live the exact opposite of the lifestyle they espoused. They did not always practice what they preached. They adopted a motto handed down from Captain Beefheart, 'Hit it to hell in the breadbasket and fingerfuck the devil', not a signal that they were about to calm down. Flea increasingly felt that he was fighting a losing battle against the drug use of Kiedis and Slovak, and despite the welcome support of an anti-drugs Irons, the other two began to slip away from the band.

Drugs affect the family of an addict in as many ways as the addict themselves – in this case the Chili Peppers as a family began to suffer badly. Kiedis enrolled at Alcoholics Anonymous, and was never secretive about his problems. Slovak, however, was. As he became more dependent on the drugs, the band distanced themselves from him, thinking it would somehow sort itself out. Flea immersed himself in other musical side projects, and got married to Loesha, whose name he had tattooed around his nipple. The lengthy schedules exacerbated the problems though, and the increasing unreliability and musical mistakes of Slovak meant it was a bedraggled and scrappy tour throughout the winter months of 1985. It is all the more astonishing then, that in these difficult and stressful circumstances, the next Red Hot Chili Peppers album was in fact to become the first step in their masterplan – a great record.

Within two months of the Red Hot Chili Peppers' third album being released, it had sold more than 'RHCP' and Freaky Styley' put together. In so doing it finally ended the major label limbo that the band had wallowed in since their initial beginnings and, although their status remained small, they were henceforth recognised as an influential and revered musical statement. At the helm of this third album, entitled 'Uplift Mofo Party Plan', was Michael Beinhorn, whose previous work with Nona Hendryx and Herbie Hancock made him a good choice, and a far preferable one to the quickly rejected Malcolm McClaren. His production methodology was far stricter than anything the band had experienced thus far, and the initial effect was a shock, but as the project developed, it became clear that Beinhorn knew exactly what he was aiming for.

When the band turned up for pre-production in January 1987 with only a meagre five songs for him to listen to, he hit the roof and furiously chastised the band for their laziness. They were sent away and told to bring back more. Despite his strict manner, he loved the same music as the Chili Peppers, bands like Fela Kuti, Hendrix, Stevie Wonder, Sly and The Family Stone, and it wasn't long before they were working together very productively. Such was Beinhorn's intent to capture the band's live sparkle and energy, he actually went on the road with them, and saw first-hand the legendary performances that by now were part of the Chili Peppers regular routine. Further to this, he spent an entire month just mixing the album to perfect the sound.

The result was an album which they believed was Step 1, the great record. It opened up whole new vistas for the

band, with more rock guitars than previously mixed with the funky wah-wah effects that gave them such a raunchy sound, and the record avoided over-playing the funk card as they had done on Clinton's second album – there was even the appearance of a sitar on 'Behind The Sun'. Rhythmically it was a beast of an album, with the occasional track subduing the song completely in the mayhem crush of bass and drums; Jack Irons in particular shone on this record.

In many sense it was a Seventies record, and the influences and familiar funk motifs were there for all to see, but the Chili Peppers gave it their own stamp, their own identity and that made it into a very powerful yet sophisticated release – it was never going to be a purist's funk record. Perhaps most importantly of all, 'The Uplift Mofo Party Plan' captured the live essence of the band, and this was probably the single most important reason why the record astounded so many people. Kiedis' lyrics were more inward looking and perceptive, maybe because of the traumatic events surrounding the band at this time, and despite the occasional foray into sexism (such as on 'No Chump Love Sucker') the lyricist maintained a compelling standard, delivered in an often ugly, but no less brilliant, jabber of a voice that gave the record yet another layer of textures. They touched on environmental concerns, satisfying people through music, spiritual mobility, sex, and social issues. And instead of the soul covers, they now recorded Bob Dylan's 22-year-old début chart hit, 'Subterranean Homesick Blues'. The Peppers wanted to be known as a hardcore psychedelic funk band, and with this album, they had hit that particular nail on the head.

When the album was released, one of the results of its success was an increasing comparison to The Beastie Boys, an observation that bewildered and annoyed the band. The lead single from the LP, 'Fight Like A Brave' was cited as musical evidence of the similarities. They had been rapping for five years now and yet some said they copied the newly formed Beastie Boys delivery. Their often loutish behaviour was also seen as further proof that they had both attended the same musical yob school, and the

final, most often voiced criticism, and probably the most offensive to the band, was that they had done to funk what The Beastie Boys had done to rap, ie imbued it with a white attitude and made it more palatable to an essentially prejudiced public. Needless to say, the Chili Peppers found all of these ideas disagreeable, and rightly so. Other criticisms voiced around this time were the same old sexist ones, as certain people failed to look past the band's superficial image and delve deeper into their music.

Since 'The Uplift Mofo Party Plan' did not actually surface until two years after the last album, the Chili Peppers had in the meantime, plenty of scope for establishing a wider live fan base. This proved to be relatively easy with their show now a raging whirlwind of activity that left each and every punter breathless. Thus, once the record was released, the band found that the album tour was sold out, and this time to much bigger venues, around 1,000 people every night – there was a notable shift in profile and recognition, still modest, but nevertheless improving. The UK as well, seemed to be at last turning on to the band, with the small tour to support the single 'Fight Like A Brave' being well received in both public and media circles alike. Supporting them in the States was a hardcore band by the name of Faith No More, and the packed crowds were treated to blistering shows night after night. In some states there were mini-riots and frenzied audience reactions resulted in police attending virtually every gig in heavy numbers. The only downer was that they were still only getting limited radio play, and after four years of hard gigging they were still only at the medium sized venues. Patience has never been a problem for the Chili Peppers however, so they carried on undaunted.

Drugs, however, have been a problem, and on this tour they became a very serious problem indeed. By now Slovak was taking in massive quantities and it was severely affecting both his health and his ability to play. Each night he would hit an increasing number of bum notes, sometimes so many the crowd would notice and grimace. Rumour swept the venues that one night he was so out of it that he played one song all evening while the rest of the band tried vainly to cover up, with obviously disastrous consequences. He looked haunted and ill, and had by now distanced himself from the rest of the group, his friends, seeking solace more and more in the drugs he fed into his weakened body. For the time being however, they had tours to complete and they had to persevere in spite of everything.

In addition, the band were now the target of abuse and criticism from right wing censorship groups that were sprouting up all over the United States during an ultra-conservative political period. Groups like the Parents Music Resource Centre campaigned angrily against the Chili Peppers' lyrics and live shows, deriding the band for sexism and obscenity when they had never even seen the group. Stickers were forced on to their record sleeves and the band were cautioned on several occasions for their outrageous live set. The track 'Party On Your Pussy' was the subject of so much complaint that EMI forced the band to change it to 'Special Secret Song' despite the band's defence that it was in their eyes a compliment to all women rather than a sexist yobbism. Not many people noticed that the less-provocatively titled 'Backwoods' was probably far more sexual, but censorship groups have never been renowned for their objectivity. To many people, the Chili Peppers were a full-frontal to the new morality and they were consequently censored at every turn during this period.

The band's defence was that music, and funk music in particular, is very sexual in nature, and that it would be sterilising it as an art form to cleanse their music, their lyrics and their act. The correlation was very direct and undeniable – Flea said parents did not want their children listening to the Chili Peppers because it was like hearing them say 'fuck'. They admitted they occasionally behaved laddishly or in a manner that was likely to cause offence, but argued that this was no reason to silence their work, which of course it was not. Maybe the band's articulation of their defence was not always the most carefully worded, such as when Flea said "we try to make music that gives you an erection" but that essentially is not the point. Against this, there was always going to be complaints against songs like 'Party On Your Pussy' and 'No Chump Love Sucker', and the Chili Peppers were unfortunate in that their reputation went before them.

When their single 'Fight Like A Brave' was released, Kiedis told the story of how when he was recording the track the rest of the band had dropped their trousers and pressed their testicles flat against the studio window to give him the inspiration for the song – many people picked up more on this tale of private behaviour than they did on the excellent song, which was by far the band's most accessible yet, a furious slab of funk and rap.

Inevitably this behaviour did not help their cause – when Jack Irons walked through British Customs with a tit-hat on his head, it proved they would never change, as he was by far the most reserved of the four. Similarly, when they told the British press their new motto was 'Rock out with your cock out!!' it confirmed for many what they had already suspected. This Californian gang-like mentality was very insular and some interpreted it as a primal, almost tribal celebration of their male sexuality – maybe it was, but there is no place for censorship of this kind and there never will be.

Despite all the controversy, the Chili Peppers incredible live shows, together with the nature of these gigs, combined to push the 'Uplift Mofo Party Plan' into the top 150 *Billboard* albums, their first chart success, where it peaked at No. 143. Again, not exactly a major breakthrough, but the content of the album and the tours that followed were sufficient to focus attention on the band and increase the expectation for their next record, scheduled to be recorded in June 1988. Unfortunately, before that next record was completed, Hillel Slovak had died of a heroin overdose.

The days leading up to this tragedy were fraught with high emotion and personal difficulty. Much against their own emotional preference, they had decided for the good of the band that they would have to sack Slovak, as his performances were by now so erratic that they were a hindrance on stage. At a Washington show the decision was finally made, and Kiedis made his way over to break the news to his old friend. As he did so, the singer with LA support band Fishbone, Angelo Moore, spotted what he was doing and intercepted Kiedis halfway. Taking him to one side, Moore pleaded with Kiedis not to sack Slovak, saying that they had to stick together and close ranks, not sack him and move on to a new guitarist. More than ever, he explained, Slovak needed the band and his friends. Kiedis himself was still using drugs heavily at this stage and maybe it was this realisation that Moore invoked that made him turn around, walk back to Flea and Jack and tell them he couldn't do it, and in fact that they shouldn't do it.

Thus, the following month, the Red Hot Chili Peppers set out on a European tour in support of the 'Abbey Road' EP, (which was released in May 1988) with Slovak still on board. The cover of this record was a pastiche of one of the most famous LP covers ever – in 1969 The Beatles had walked across the pedestrian crossing in NW10 near the famous studio with Paul McCartney wearing no socks or shoes. Nineteen years later the Red Hot Chili Peppers did exactly the same, only this time with nothing on *but* for socks, again placed over the band's genitalia. It was a brilliantly hilarious cover and the photo earned the band press and publicity beyond anything they could have imagined. The lead track was a wild version of Hendrix's 'Fire' which had originally been recorded for the second album 'Freaky Styley' but was left off the final cut. When the band hit Europe to tour the EP the crowds went mad, but unfortunately many were again more interested in their socks than their music. Even so, it was easily their best ever tour, and the progress was escalated considerably. Their preference for nudity was further displayed at a festival in Finland when they made an impromptu appearance at the start of The Ramones' set completely naked but for their by now well-worn socks. The Ramones were not amused but the crowd loved it, as did the press. Once this highly successful tour was over, the band returned to Los Angeles to begin the next album – but within four weeks Slovak was dead. He was 25.

The Red Hot Chili Peppers had been through all manner of traumas and controversies until now, and had come through them all – but to actually lose a member of the band because of their outrageous and wild lifestyles was a blow that was barely incomprehensible. Kiedis and Flea were devastated, and their initial feelings of guilt for thinking of sacking Slovak compounded their grief. Kiedis vanished for weeks, hiding out in a small Mexican village where he dried out completely. Flea was not even sure if he would ever see Kiedis again, let alone whether he would still be in the band. But it was Slovak's longtime friend Jack Irons who lost control totally when he heard of the death. Irons withdrew completely from everyday life, avoiding at all costs anything to do with the band. No rehearsals, no practice on his own, he wouldn't even answer the phone in case it was someone wanting to talk about the band. He began to hate the band and what it had done to his best friend and gradually he made up his mind never to play drums again. By this stage however, he had lost his mental stability and was subsequently admitted to a mental hospital for treatment. His collapse and Slovak's death heralded what was the probable end of the Chili Peppers.

Kiedis regrouped, cleaned up and gained some order in his life. Flea's wife gave birth to a baby girl, and gradually, but slowly, they began to regain some normality in their lives. The question was 'could they ever replace the two original members?' The death of Slovak weighed particularly heavily on their minds, and for some time it was unclear if they could ever carry on. Eventually however, they vowed to pursue their career in the Red Hot Chili Peppers, if nothing else for the memory of Slovak. Irons eventually joined Joe Strummer's band for a US tour and recorded guitar work for the album 'Earthquake Weather' and then later toured with snot punksters Red Cross as well, but his time with the Chili Peppers was over.

If the band had any future, the two founder members had to find replacements, which was no easy matter, as they had always been based on close personal kinship. When Kiedis was taking so many drugs that it affected his creativity and personality, Flea had become disgruntled and unhappy and even told him he couldn't play music together with him any more, yet they had come through that closer than ever. The two players they recruited finally were Duane Blackbyrd McKnight, an ex-George Clinton guitarist, and Darren D.H. Peligro, former drummer for The Dead Kennedys, so their new members came highly qualified. They resurfaced

publically in September 1988 on the MTV 120 Minutes show; however, despite the excellent backgrounds of the two new members, the chemistry was not right and within a matter of weeks they were both sacked. Thus started a long and difficult search for ideal replacements that took the Chili Peppers a full five years to complete.

John Frusciante was 15 when he first saw The Red Hot Chili Peppers and he was immediately hooked. He started buying up all their records and learning them all by heart, memorising the amazing guitar work of Hillel Slovak precisely. He left home so that he might be able to follow the band more closely, and became something of a fanatic in the true sense – it is doubtful whether the band had a more devoted musical fan among their burgeoning ranks of supporters. They became friends with Frusciante because he appeared at every show, and when they heard of his superb guitar skills they recommended that he audition for the guitar role in the band Thelonius Monster, a popular West Coast act.

Because of Frusciante's lack of confidence to audition for such a big band, Kiedis and Flea decided to escort him to the studio and they sat in the corner while he played. As he did their eyes met and then they looked across at Thelonius Monster who were clearly thinking the same thing. When John had finished, they walked over to him and said 'You're in..." Frusciante could not believe his luck – him, in Thelonius Monster! He could hardly believe his ears when the Monster's' singer then finished his sentence – 'The Red Hot Chili Peppers that is!!!'

The assembled musicians could hardly believe how well John played, and it was immediately apparent that he was absolutely ideal for the Chili Peppers, so perfectly had he copied Slovak's style and work that he was almost a natural for the part. It was an uncanny stroke of luck for both parties. Frusciante did not tell them that he had never played with any other musicians before. Now they only had to find a drummer. Auditions started very slowly and they were becoming disillusioned with the whole tedious process. They were down to the last man for the day, when in walked 26-year-old Chad Smith, who had not even heard of the Chili Peppers, but who proceeded to deliver a blitzkrieg on his drum kit, screaming obscenities at the top of his voice as he played. Along with John, the Chili Peppers were now a completed line-up once again, and in March 1989, nine months after Slovak's death, they did what they knew best – hit the road.

It was on these dates that Kiedis was arrested for sexual battery and indecent exposure, after an incident at George Mason University. Backstage after the show, he had allegedly dropped his trousers in front of a female fan and then pulled them back up before retiring to the dressing room. He was therefore shocked when he was charged the next day with such serious offences, in fact any offence at all. A year later he was convicted and fined a sum in the region of $1,000 for each offence, the sexual battery charge being the most serious. Ironically, elsewhere on this tour, Kiedis was the paragon of virtue. He was in love with actress Ione Skye and he gave up his womanising, as well as alcohol, cigarettes and drugs, a massive and impressive attempt at a huge lifestyle change in one big step, and Kiedis seemed quite capable of managing it.

The set on this tour was a bombardment of sound and rhythm with crest after crest of super-charged fusions between funk and rock. Kiedis and Flea would bait the crowd and increase the frenetic atmosphere inside the venues before baring their souls in true life confessions and stories. The expectations for the next album were fuelled by these dates and the band knew if they produced a strong record they would be in a very favourable position, despite the tragedies they had only recently suffered.

With Michael Beinhorn again at the controls, the record, entitled 'Mother's Milk', was completed by the spring of 1989, and released in the autumn of the same year. The nature of the band's previous releases demanded that this record promote the 'song' as the absolute priority, as they had occasionally deferred its importance to secondary behind the bewildering rhythm section which pivoted around the mighty bass playing of Flea. If the band were to truly progress and utilise the solid live following they had worked so hard to earn, they had to write an album that was melodically more inviting, while retaining the power and dynamism of the earlier records. It had to be more musical. Kiedis summed up this challenge aptly as they recorded the album: "The thing we're trying to do is strike a groove that defies all categories and transcends all mortal ties, standing on its own as great music, like a few people, Bob Marley, John Lennon, Miles Davis, have done."

The album featured eleven original compositions and two cover versions, Stevie Wonder's 'Higher Ground' and Jimi Hendrix's 'Fire' which featured Hillel Slovak on guitar (one of his impressionist paintings could also be admired on the back cover). Flea played trumpet on the three tracks 'Taste The Pain', 'Pretty Little Ditty' and 'Subway To Venus' and in all, the record offered exactly the style of musical progression that the band had needed. Appropriately the first single taken for the record was a tribute to Slovak called 'Knock Me Down' and its warm reception gave the band an idea of the enormous success that this album was about to enjoy.

The record sold massively and put them into the top flight of the album charts, while their singles and tours started to sell out rapidly, as did their t-shirts and merchandise (including one showing Madonna masturbating to The Red Hot Chili Peppers). 'Mother's Milk' finally gave the Peppers the recognition they deserved and had been looking for all these years.

The success was strengthened by the excellent tours the band played, despite scrubbing plans to tour with Aerosmith. No drugs were allowed on the road as the band reacted vigilantly to the deaths and illness caused by these distractions in the past. The new direction worked – in Europe they headlined a massive festival in Amsterdam's Dam Square and found themselves the subject of a media frenzy across their own continent as well as abroad. With them on the road they took Clip Payne of Parliament backing vocals fame, and Keith Chapman on saxophone, so in all it was a mighty set up. Kiedis' famous acrobatics were now so daring that he frequently left the stage battered and bruised from his antics, and in one case he was hobbling around on crutches all day before the show, only to transform for the actual gig into a cartwheeling maniac gymnast. The painful swelling and severe bruising the following day was the price he gladly paid for pulling off an amazing show.

Even though they were more careful with their habits on this tour, there were still more incidents and controversy surrounding the shows than most bands manage in a whole career. In the UK they demanded to play the Jonathan Ross show naked, and when that was refused, they only agreed to play at all if Flea was suspended upside down for the entire performance. In Green Bay they were arrested for indecent exposure again but let off after police were persuaded by the band's manager that it was all in high spirits. When the band went on to the MTV Spring Break Party they started dancing with a bikini clad audience member, and Flea picked her up on his back and spun her around while Chad spanked her bottom. They all then fell over into a heap and Flea allegedly simulated sex with the girl lying in front of him. He was later charged with various misdemeanours, and unfortunately this occurred the same week as Kiedis' battery conviction was announced.

If the censors wanted any further grounds to criticise the band they had plenty here, but by now America wanted to hear and see as much of The Red Hot Chili Peppers that they were in the more powerful position and could ride out the storm. This new found popularity was reflected in the band's contribution to the block-busting Hollywood smash *Pretty Woman* soundtrack ('Show Me Your Soul'). When they occasionally ran off the rails on this tour, instead of derogatory and damaging press criticism, the band became the subject of a media frenzy, so much so that when Flea and Frusciante joined an ad hoc punk band called Hate, they had to call off the whole fun project because they had attracted too much attention. With the subsequent singles 'Higher Ground' and 'Taste The Pain' (a UK Top 30 hit) being similar successes, the album 'Mother's Milk' finally succeeded in elevating the Chili Peppers from the grasp of popular obscurity to the international limelight. A second series of dates saw them play venues such as Red Rocks and other massive arenas. The Chili Peppers' time had come.

When a band experiences the degree of success that the Chili Peppers did on the 'Mother's Milk' project, it is only a matter of time before major record labels start sniffing around, regardless of whether that band already has a record deal or not. The period after the band's fifth album saw a veritable corporate scramble for their signatures after they announced that they would be leaving EMI in search of more understanding quarters. In true Chili Peppers fashion they signed to Sony and even had photographs taken with the company President, then at the very last minute switched to Warners, after a personal phone call to each one of them from the President of Warners, Mo Ostin. Nobody can say the band ever do anything straightforwardly! The deal with Warners was rumoured to be in the region of $10 million, a massive amount, but one that the company were confident they could recoup now that the Chili Peppers were recognised as one of the country's top acts.

The band chose Rick Rubin, Def Jam mainman, as the producer for their next album. Instead of heading for a mega-bucks studio he took them to a rented hacienda out of town and hired the studio gear in. He told them to make no arrangements for the next two months and that they would effectively be isolated from the rest of the world while recording took place. As if this wasn't unusual enough, they heard strange noises and felt a weird presence in the house and called in a psychic who confirmed their suspicions – the house was in fact haunted. The band decided (against the advice of the mediums) that the ghosts were friendly and completed the recording of the album regardless. They hired an ex-Playboy centrefold as the resident cook and also their own security men. Because the tracks were recorded live, Rubin managed to capture the organic sound of the band at its best. The one cover version, Robert Johnson's 'They're Red Hot' was recorded outside behind the hacienda with the traffic roaring past. This was indicative of the nature of the whole sessions – fortunately the unusual, even odd circumstances worked.

'Bloodsugarsexmagik' was in short, a colossal international smash. It stayed in the US *Billboard* charts for over a year and earned platinum status. The band were featured on every magazine cover, including *Rolling Stone* and every date on the mammoth world tour was sold out The Red Hot Chili Peppers were catapulted to the very heights of international music. It was in many ways a crude album with elements of sex and death, but the Chili Peppers had long since given up making excuses or explaining themselves (besides, of the 17 tracks here, only two or three were overtly sexual). Their music was now so powerful it was a justification in itself. In the aftermath of the Chili Peppers there were already many musical derivatives of their unique sound, but none quite so sparkling as the original. With this album the band finally delivered the ultimate on record, surpassing even the remarkable 'Mother's Milk'.

As if to cement the critical acclaim that was heaped upon 'Bloodsugarsexmagik' the Chili Peppers singles from the album further escalated their status. 'Give It Away' was perhaps the punchiest track on the record, and received such massive radio airplay it made a mockery of the short-sighted playlists which had excluded the band until so recently. Furthermore, the song's video went on in September 1992 to win MTV's award for Best Breakthrough Video – Step 2 accomplished. The next single 'Under The Bridge', an account of Kiedis' dangerous liaisons with the seedy underworld of drugs saw the band's acclaim soar to new heights – it was perhaps understandable for such a turbo-charged band that their slowest track won them the final and complete acceptance of the mainstream, rather than one of their breakneck numbers.

1992 brought even more success for the band. Despite fighting off a ludicrous law suit by a model claiming they had allegedly used parts of her body without authorisation for the cover of 'Mother's Milk', the band enjoyed a year of great success. In Britain, the music public finally took to them, their shows at the Brixton Academy could have sold out many times over, and the press at last recognised their unique talent. The only blemish on this visit to the UK was their being refused a performance on *Top Of The Pops* because they insisted on playing in Victorian drag and in the words of a programme official 'taking the piss'.

Back in America they toured with Pearl Jam, as well as Nirvana and The Smashing Pumpkins as they joined the wave of alternative bands taking the world by storm – in some territories, including Australasia, Chilimania appeared to have been born. Step 3 was consequently achieved – a great tour. It seemed perfectly natural that they should then be asked to headline the prestigious Lollapalooza 2 tour, the second in a recession beating package that included phenomenal band line-ups, including the likes of Ministry, Ice Cube, Soundgarden, Jesus & Mary Chain, and Pearl Jam, providing an ambitious and iconoclastic mix of genres. After years struggling it seemed the Chili Peppers could do no wrong. Then as the world tour arrived in Japan, John Frusciante announced that he was leaving and that after the next show he would fly home. It was the band's most successful year so far. Lollapalooza 2, the peak of their live career thus far, was but three weeks away.

Frusciante had simply become disillusioned with the stresses and strains of being in a touring, working band, and never accepted or appreciated the fame and personal recognition that his job brought him. He wanted to play in smaller clubs than the 5,000-plus seaters that were now the Chili Peppers bread and butter. He wanted to be able to play for other small-time bands. He didn't want to do the endless rounds of press and TV interviews and record company obligations and all that comes with being in a superband. He could not tolerate it any longer. Despite the bad timing, the split was not acrimonious, but nevertheless the Chili Peppers were left with the unenviable task of recruiting a new guitarist only 20 days before the mammoth 27 date Lollapalooza 2 tour started. The lucky man chosen was Arik Marshall, formerly of Los Angeles band Marshall Law, who rehearsed for five hours every day for the next three weeks. His first gig with the Chili Peppers was in front of 60,000 at the San Francisco Shoreline Amphitheatre. Amazingly, he said he was less scared of the huge crowd than he was of the flame throwing helmets the Chili's had taken to wearing on stage!!! A baptism of fire indeed.

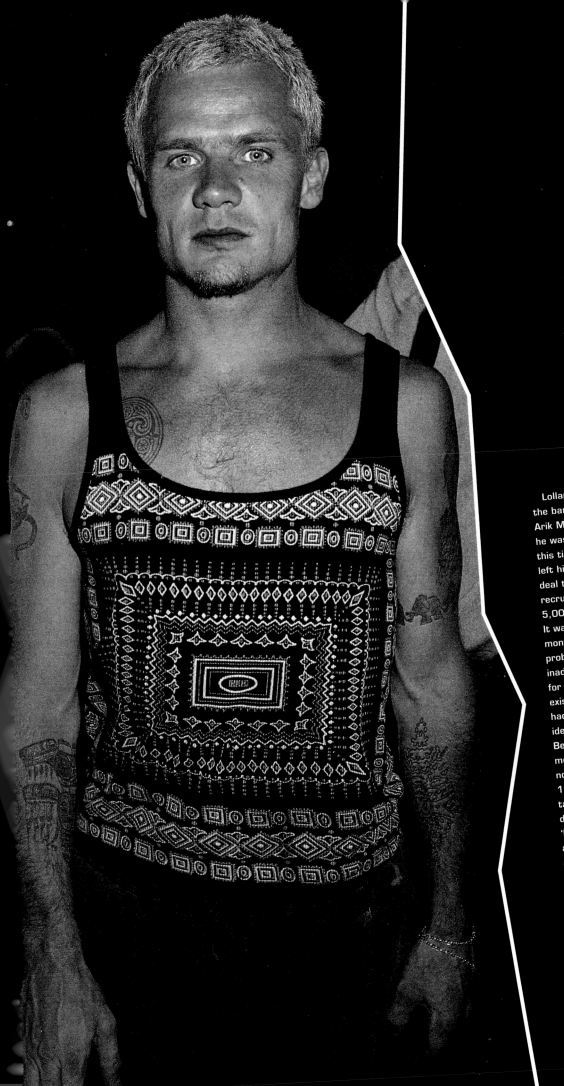

Lollapalooza 2 was a total success for the band – unfortunately the new recruit Arik Marshall was not, and shortly after he was replaced by yet another new face, this time the youngster Jesse Tobias, who left his own band on the verge of a record deal to play with the Peppers (he was recruited after a newspaper advert drew 5,000 callers in the first day alone). It was not a wise choice, and within two months he also was asked to leave. The problem was that the band were perhaps inadvertently looking for a replacement for Hillel Slovak, when no such player existed. He could not be replaced; they had to look for someone with their own identity and style and rebuild from that. Before they found him, they enjoyed yet more huge success when they were nominated for eight awards at the MTV 1992 Annual Award Ceremony, eventually taking home three awards for two different tracks ('Give It Away' and 'Under The Bridge') ahead of bands such as U2, Eric Clapton, Queen, Pearl Jam and Prince. Similar success was enjoyed at the next year's Grammy Awards as well – so much for funk music being unfashionable. The Chili Peppers had by now almost single-handedly re-introduced a discarded musical form into the mainstream marketplace.

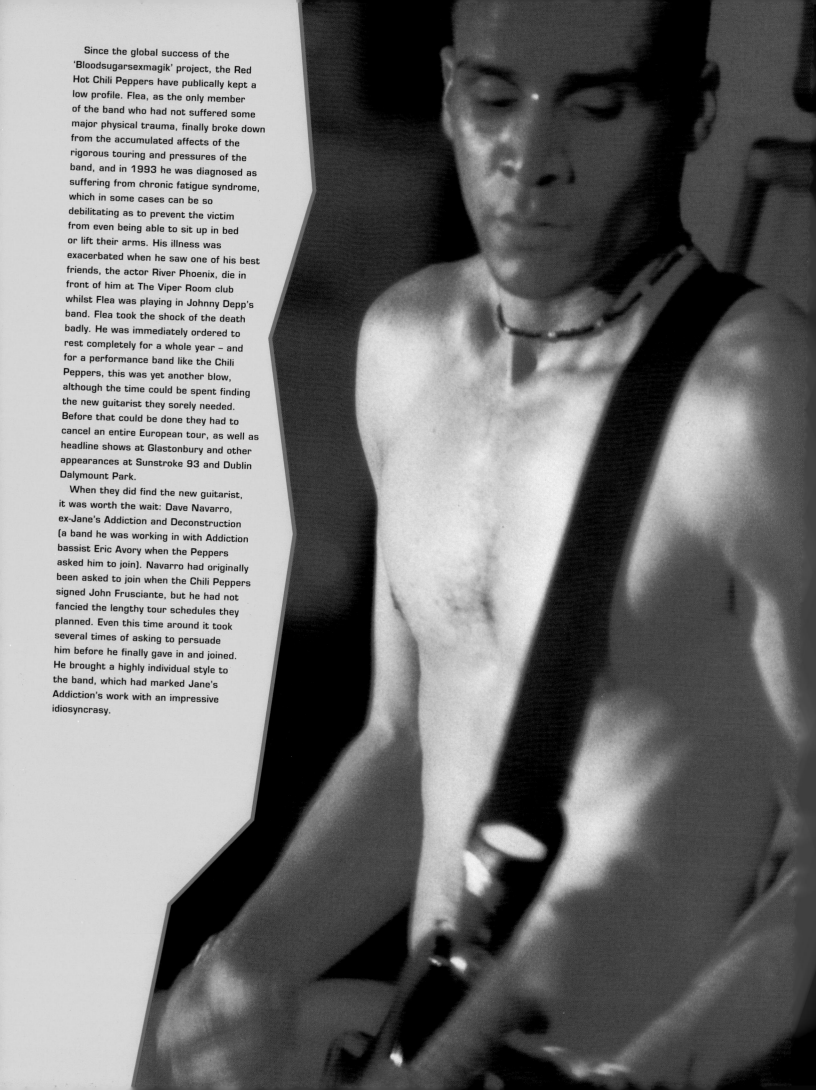

Since the global success of the 'Bloodsugarsexmagik' project, the Red Hot Chili Peppers have publically kept a low profile. Flea, as the only member of the band who had not suffered some major physical trauma, finally broke down from the accumulated affects of the rigorous touring and pressures of the band, and in 1993 he was diagnosed as suffering from chronic fatigue syndrome, which in some cases can be so debilitating as to prevent the victim from even being able to sit up in bed or lift their arms. His illness was exacerbated when he saw one of his best friends, the actor River Phoenix, die in front of him at The Viper Room club whilst Flea was playing in Johnny Depp's band. Flea took the shock of the death badly. He was immediately ordered to rest completely for a whole year – and for a performance band like the Chili Peppers, this was yet another blow, although the time could be spent finding the new guitarist they sorely needed. Before that could be done they had to cancel an entire European tour, as well as headline shows at Glastonbury and other appearances at Sunstroke 93 and Dublin Dalymount Park.

When they did find the new guitarist, it was worth the wait: Dave Navarro, ex-Jane's Addiction and Deconstruction (a band he was working in with Addiction bassist Eric Avory when the Peppers asked him to join). Navarro had originally been asked to join when the Chili Peppers signed John Frusciante, but he had not fancied the lengthy tour schedules they planned. Even this time around it took several times of asking to persuade him before he finally gave in and joined. He brought a highly individual style to the band, which had marked Jane's Addiction's work with an impressive idiosyncrasy.

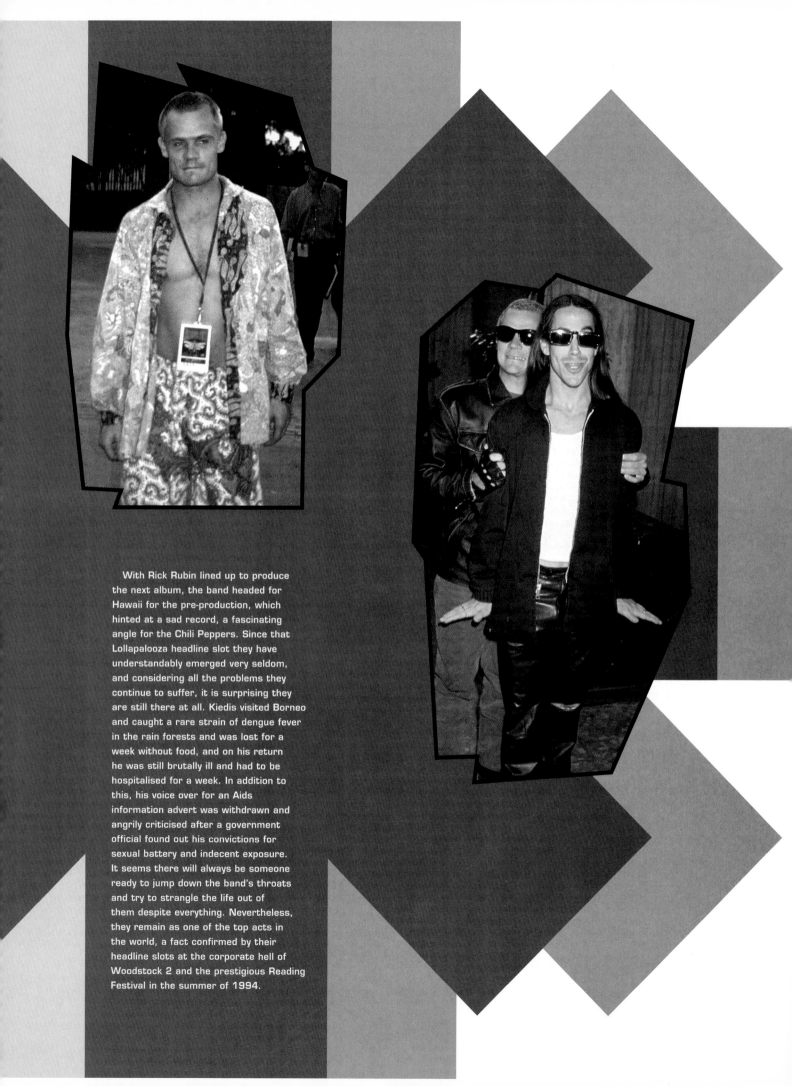

With Rick Rubin lined up to produce
the next album, the band headed for
Hawaii for the pre-production, which
hinted at a sad record, a fascinating
angle for the Chili Peppers. Since that
Lollapalooza headline slot they have
understandably emerged very seldom,
and considering all the problems they
continue to suffer, it is surprising they
are still there at all. Kiedis visited Borneo
and caught a rare strain of dengue fever
in the rain forests and was lost for a
week without food, and on his return
he was still brutally ill and had to be
hospitalised for a week. In addition to
this, his voice over for an Aids
information advert was withdrawn and
angrily criticised after a government
official found out his convictions for
sexual battery and indecent exposure.
It seems there will always be someone
ready to jump down the band's throats
and try to strangle the life out of
them despite everything. Nevertheless,
they remain as one of the top acts in
the world, a fact confirmed by their
headline slots at the corporate hell of
Woodstock 2 and the prestigious Reading
Festival in the summer of 1994.

Despite the image of four half naked yobs engaged in moronic embraces, pulling faces, dropping their trousers and taking drugs, drink and womanising to new extremes, the Red Hot Chili Peppers have consistently managed to produce records that have surprised, challenged and intrigued thousands, and eventually millions, of listeners. Their frenetic live shows set new records in hyperactivity and their uncompromising musical integrity never waivers. The taut basslines, even tauter muscles, tattoos, hair and socks are all part of the compulsive presentation of a band that have endured difficulties that few bands even come close to, and yet they have persevered throughout.

They might be self-contradictory at times, even hypocritical, but they only ask to be judged on their music, their soul music. They quickly learnt that waving their dicks in people's faces might not be everyone's idea of a great night out, but that never extinguished their sense of the melodramatic, even though at times this has been utterly unintentional. Their eclectic and energetic approach avoids the sycophantic plagiarism of other less reputable bands, and continues to cut a path through musical barriers across the world with its melting pot barrage of funk rhythms, rock power, mixed with a jazz and rap ideology. As a perfect caricature of a rock and roll myth, it should come as no surprise to anyone that they have been approached to make a film about their story. They always have been, they still are and they always will be, the stuff of Hollywood. But without the music there would be none of this. And that is what the Red Hot Chili Peppers are all about – soul music.